To:

D1359980

Illustrations copyright © 2011 Steve Haskamp
Designed by David Cole Wheeler

Copyright © 2011
Peter Pauper Press, Inc.
202 Mamaroneck Avenue
White Plains, NY 10601

ISBN 978-1-4413-0520-6

Printed in China
7 6 5 4 3 2 1

Visit us at www.peterpauper.com

Dream Big

Introduction

"Commencement" means "beginning," and as you launch into this next chapter of your life's adventure, take this little book along for navigation and inspiration.

Wisdom and humor from the likes of J. K. Rowling, The Dalai Lama, Bill Gates, Stephen Colbert, and a host of other famous and not-so-famous folk, encourage you to **Dream Big**.

Follow your heart as you blaze your own path. Learn and love large as you create your remarkable life.

Congratulations!

It takes courage to grow up and become who you really are.

e. e. cummings

Don't feel guilty if you don't know what you want to do with your life. The most interesting people I know didn't know at 22 what they wanted to do with their lives. Some of the most interesting 40-year-olds I know still don't.

Mary Schmich

You cannot help but learn more as you take the world into your hands. Take it up reverently, for it is an old piece of clay, with millions of thumbprints on it.

John Updike

Find a partner to love and
a job you adore so much
you would do for free—
although you really do have to
demand that they pay you.

Gail Collins

An education goes a long way toward putting you at the controls of your life, an actor rather than acted upon.

Ray Suarez

Tend to your dream and
sing your song. That song is there
to educate us, it's there to hold
our hands, it's there to entertain us
and nourish us in the best
and worst of times.

Wynton Marsalis

Life is like one big Mardi Gras,
but instead of showing your
boobs, show people your brain,
and if they like what they see,
you'll have more beads than
you know what to do with.

Ellen DeGeneres

Imagine

We do not need magic
to change the world;
we carry all the power we need
inside ourselves already:
We have the power
to imagine better.

J. K. Rowling

Your time is limited, so don't
waste it living someone else's life . . . .
Don't let the noise of others'
opinions drown out your own inner voice.
And most important,
have the courage to follow
your heart and intuition.
They somehow already know
what you truly want to become.

Steve Jobs

You are your own stories and therefore free to imagine and experience what it means to be human . . . without reinventing the hatreds you learned in the sandbox. And although you don't have complete control over the narrative (no author does, I can tell you), you could nevertheless create it.

Toni Morrison

The best advice I can give
anybody about going out
into the world is this:
Don't do it. I have been
out there. It is a mess.

Russell Baker

A good person
means someone with a good heart,
a sense of caring for the welfare
of others, a sense of commitment,
a sense of responsibility.
Education and the warm heart,
the compassion heart—if you combine
these two, then your education
and knowledge will be constructive.
Then you are yourself on the way
to becoming a happy person.

The Dalai Lama

Now is the time in your life
to be selfish. To explore.
To take chances. Remember
being selfish is not the same as
being self-indulgent. You have
the gift of time. Use it to do
what you love. Believe anything
is possible and then work
like hell to make it happen.

Julianna Margulies

Explore

Your power is born of experiment and the endless grudge match between fear and hope. You could close your eyes and wait for this moment to pass or hoard canned goods. . . . But if you go outside and walk around, you'll find the parcels of grace, of ingenuity and enterprise—people riding change like a skateboard.

Nancy Gibbs

Your dreams, what you hope for and all that, it's not separate from your life. It grows right up out of it.

Barbara Kingsolver

Uncertainty

is not a problem,
so long as we do not allow it
to immobilize us. It's not that
we're lacking ideas, if anything we
are burdened by an abundance
of possibilities. We must seize
this uncertainty, relish in it.
But eventually, we
must make a choice.

Alexander Atkins

We're very mobile.
We have to learn to create
community and [choose] community
wherever we are, wherever we move to.
[We have] to volunteer, to be of service,
to vote and to take leadership seriously.
It's not enough to work in a business,
or in government or in a nonprofit.
Each of us has an obligation to be
a community leader as well.

Lynn Luckow

Savor

If you want a life of duty, and of responsibility and of decency, you will pursue happiness. Not enjoyment, not fun, not pleasure, though these are all aspects of happiness, but a life of happiness in all its complexity and contradictions. Likewise if you want to be happy, you'll do your duties with joy, you'll see your responsibilities as gifts, and you'll understand decency as a simple human thing called love.

Abigail Disney

Remember to enjoy your lives.
Take risks while you can.
Never be afraid to ask for
what you want. . . . Never let
the fear of not knowing what will
happen deter you from trying.
It's the things that we don't
expect that make life interesting.

Christine Chai

Perseverance—

or what some will simply call
"stick-to-it-iveness"—goes hand
in hand with a choice
to follow your passion and not
simply dollar signs as you pursue
your career and life goals.

Phillip Bosco

My favorite animal is the turtle.
The reason is that in order for the
turtle to move, it has to stick
its neck out. There are going to be
times in your life when you're going
to have to stick your neck out.
There will be challenges and
instead of hiding in a shell,
you have to go out
and meet them!

Ruth Westheimer

Persistence is critical.
Being creative and persistent
is even better. . . . Be fearless.
Have the courage to take risks.
Go where there are no guarantees.
Get out of your comfort zone,
even if it means being
uncomfortable.

Katie Couric

Believe that the sort of life you wish to live is, at this very moment, just waiting for you to summon it up. And when you wish for it, you begin moving toward it, and it, in turn, begins moving toward you.

Suzan-Lori Parks

If you want to play a game, go to where it's played and find a way to get in. Things happen when you get in the game.

Chris Matthews

Find the smartest people you can and surround yourself with them. You will be challenged to do your best and they would elevate your thinking. Smart people will challenge you to think harder and in entirely different ways. Search criticism to become a better self.

Marissa Mayers

Know yourself and to your own self be true. You may find some day three or four years from now that you simply don't like engineering, or teaching, or architecture, or government, or the company you started with. . . . At that point you have to muster whatever self-confidence you have, and every bit of your courage, and make the decision to do something else with your life. It is always better sooner than later to make that call.

David L. Calhoun

*Believe in yourself
and you'll do just fine.
And, oh yes, don't then
forget to market yourself
and your ideas. Use both
sides of your brain.*

Michael Uslan

Never give in. Never give in.
Never, never, never, never—
in nothing, great or small,
large or petty—never give in,
except to convictions of honor
and good sense.

Winston Churchill

Listen once in a while.
It's amazing what you can hear.
On a hot summer day in the country
you can hear the corn growing, the crack
of a tin roof buckling under the
power of the sun. . . . Or sometimes when
you're talking up a storm so brilliant,
so charming that you can hardly believe
how wonderful you are, pause just a moment
and listen to yourself. It's good for the soul
to hear yourself as others hear you,
and next time maybe, just maybe,
you will not talk so much, so loudly,
so brilliantly, so charmingly,
so utterly shamefully foolishly.

Russell Baker

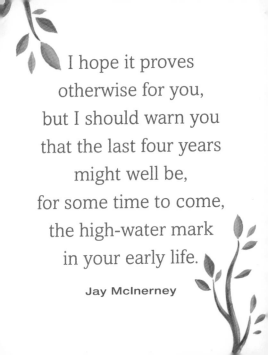

I hope it proves
otherwise for you,
but I should warn you
that the last four years
might well be,
for some time to come,
the high-water mark
in your early life.

Jay McInerney

One of my biggest memories of Harvard came in January 1975, when I made a call from Currier House to a company in Albuquerque that had begun making the world's first personal computers. I offered to sell them software.

I worried that they would realize I was just a student in a dorm and hang up on me. Instead they said: "We're not quite ready, come see us in a month," which was a good thing, because we hadn't written the software yet.

From that moment, I worked day and night on this little extra credit project that marked the end of my college education and the beginning of a remarkable journey with Microsoft.

Bill Gates

No matter how much potential you think you have, a little humility will serve you well—and help you focus on doing your best in the job you've got, rather than plotting to get the job you think you deserve.

Katie Couric

No matter what you choose to do, know
that you have the ability—each one of you—
to write the next chapter in America's story.
Starting your careers in troubled times is
a challenge, but it's also a privilege. . . .
It's times like the one you're facing today
that force us to try harder and dig deeper. . . .
These are the tasks lying before you,
and I have no doubt all of you are
up to the challenge.

Barack Obama

If I can leave you with one thought today at this critical juncture in your lives and that of the world, it would be to hold to your true selves. Realize the tremendous opportunities available to you and trust in yourselves as you use individual ingenuity to define your life and role in the world.

Robert Redford

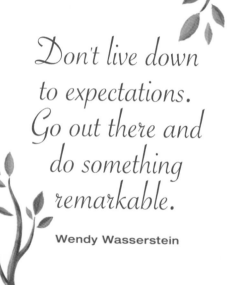

Don't live down to expectations. Go out there and do something remarkable.

Wendy Wasserstein

Do not follow where the path
may lead. Go, instead,
where there is no path
and leave a trail.

Ralph Waldo Emerson

Be who you are and
say what you feel
because those who mind
don't matter and those
who matter don't mind.

Dr. Seuss

At commencement
you wear your square-shaped
mortarboards.
My hope is that from
time to time you will
let your minds be bold,
and wear sombreros.

Paul Freund

I know one other thing for certain as well. No graduating class gets to choose the world they graduate into. Every class has its own unique challenges. Every class enters a history that up to that point has been written for them. And your generation is no different. But what is different about your generation is the chance that each of you has to take history into your own hands and write it larger.

Joe Biden

A graduation ceremony is an event where the commencement speaker tells thousands of students dressed in identical caps and gowns that "individuality" is the key to success.

Robert Orben

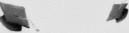

Don't waste time learning the "tricks of the trade." Instead, learn the trade.

James Charlton

Success

is the ability
to go from one failure
to another with no
loss of enthusiasm.

Winston Churchill

*There are no shortcuts
to any place worth going.*

Beverly Sills

There is a good reason
they call these ceremonies
"commencement exercises."
Graduation is not the end;
it's the beginning.

Orrin Hatch

You are educated.
Your certification is
in your degree.
You may think of it as
the ticket to the good life.
Let me ask you to think of
an alternative. Think of it
as your ticket to
change the world.

Tom Brokaw

Twenty years from now
you will be more disappointed
by the things you didn't do
than by the ones you did.
So throw off the bowlines,
sail away from the safe harbor.
Catch the trade winds in your sails.
Explore. Dream. Discover.

Mark Twain

Today, perhaps more than ever,
philosophy and imagination
are not luxuries. They are not
just personal pleasures or college
electives. They are survival skills,
and we ignore them at our peril.
I urge you to remember that
and not to slight your dreams
or your inner lives in the rush
of jobs and real estate.

Marvin Bell

Make the world before you
a better one by going into it with
all boldness. You are up to it and
you are fit for it; you deserve it
and if you make your own best
contribution, the world before you
will become a bit more
deserving of you.

Seamus Heaney

In school, grades and test results measure accomplishment. You know what is expected and where you stand. But once you leave school, you will have to rely upon an inner compass, for only you can set the standards by which your sense of purpose will compete against temptations, distractions, and confusions. You will often be uncertain, for the path to a life of fulfillment and accomplishment is nowhere clearly marked.

Madeleine K. Albright

Life takes its own turns, makes its own demands, writes its own story. And along the way, we start to realize we are not the author. We begin to understand that life is ours to live, but not to waste, and that the greatest rewards are found in the commitments we make with our whole hearts—to the people we love and to the causes that earn our sacrifices. I hope that each of you will know these rewards. I hope you will find them in your own way and your own time.

George W. Bush

Remember to always ask questions: no question is too stupid. You're not as smart as you think you are. You never will be. There's always room to learn. Don't be scared to ask.

Meredith Vieira

Really, when you think about it,
failure in life is inevitable.
It is going to happen unless of
course you live your life so
carefully that you very well
may have never lived at all.
And if that is the case, then
you have already failed.

Jonathan Youshaei

Follow your passion and your heart.
You will not find it in things or money
because the more you have the
more you will use that as a metric
and to get more. The important things
are those that fill you from inside.
It will be grounded in people,
in your relationship
with people.

Randy Pausch

As you start your journey,
the first thing you should do is
throw away that store-bought map
and begin to draw your own.
And don't spend so much time
trying to choose the perfect opportunity
that you miss the right opportunity.
Recognize that there will be failures,
and acknowledge that there will be
obstacles. But you will learn from
your mistakes and the mistakes
of others, for there is very little
learning in success.

Michael S. Dell

And if someone does
offer you a job, say yes.
You can always quit later.
Then at least you'll be one of
the unemployed as opposed
to one of the never-
employed. Nothing looks
worse on a resume than
nothing. So, say "yes."
In fact, say "yes"
as often as you can.

Stephen Colbert

The fireworks begin today. Each diploma is a lighted match. Each one of you is a fuse.

Edward Koch

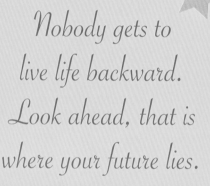

Nobody gets to live life backward. Look ahead, that is where your future lies.

Ann Landers

For a long time it had seemed
to me that life was about to begin—
real life. But there was always
some obstacle in the way,
something to be gotten through
first, some unfinished business,
time still to be served,
a debt to be paid.
Then life would begin.
At last it dawned on me that
these obstacles were my life.

Alfred D. Souza

Soar

Never give in to pessimism.
Don't know that you can't fly,
and you will soar like an eagle.
Don't end up regretting what
you did not do because you were
too lazy or too frightened to soar.
Be a bumblebee!
And soar to the heavens.
You can do it.

Earl Bakken

Learning is the best antidote
to and against ignorance
and fanaticism and hatred. . . .
Learning is an antidote because
when we learn, no matter who
we are and where we come from,
we still are marveling at the beauty
of a sentence or cadence by
Shakespeare, or an idea by Plato.
Learning, therefore, is what brings
people together. Continue to learn.

Elie Wiesel

Work diligently, but don't deprive
yourself of a good night's sleep.
Slow down enough to notice the
blooming things. And even though
you may be planting teeny little
starter plants in your garden,
space them far enough apart
so that they have plenty
of room to grow.
The same goes for you.

Anne Hill

We all need to be given opportunities, and then we have to disregard all of the statistics that predict we're not likely to reach our goal. Put blinders on to those things that conspire to hold you back, especially the ones in your own head. Guard your good mood. Listen to music every day, joke, and love and read more for fun, especially poetry.

Meryl Streep

Commencement speeches were invented largely in the belief that outgoing college students should never be released into the world until they have been properly sedated.

Garry Trudeau

Education

is our passport
to the future, for tomorrow
belongs to the people
who prepare for it today.

Malcolm X

Keep your circle of acquaintances wide so that you will always have fresh points of view. Listen to your critics, and if you can't answer them well, maybe they have something. I pray that you will worry, if you start sounding like everybody else you know.

Jane Bryant Quinn

Expect to change things.
Expect to be willing
to work hard.
Expect to practice virtue.
Expect to show compassion.
Expect to keep our nation
second to none.
Expect to be the next
Greatest Generation.

Anthony Mullen